Shac

By

Anna Maria Mickiewicz

Cover designed by Sandra Simonds (photo), Anna Maria Mickiewicz and Steve Cawte

photos of Great Britain (Devon, London, Cornwall): made by Anna Maria Mickiewicz

ISBN: *978-1-915819-83-3*

I dedicate the book to my beloved late son Stanislaw Satn Mickiewicz (1986-2023)

OTHER TITLES BY IMPSPIRED

Maybury –
by Mary Farrell

Polygon -
by Domonique

Leviathan –
by Jae Jenkins Scott

Hyperbola -
by Shelly Norris

Spun Tales and Woven Words –
by North Coast Writers

The Mining Muse –
by Marc Darnell

Apartmentalized –
by Dan Flore III

CONTENTS

desert rain in london

i long for a radiant rain
rain of salvation
field rain

a spruce smells dry
it has died forgotten
the light of the city breaks through the dusk

we run away thirsty
there is no chill on a damp morning
asking the goddess Hora for grace
for the rhythm of nature

is it Spring or Summer?
the desert air blurs my eyes

London, in May

secret of the manuscript in oxford

we rise
clothed in clouds
lavender roses fountains
under the spell
 of ancient courtyards
we enter along jagged blue mosaics
 stumble on the voices
 of angelic Goths
we bid farewell to medieval walls
open up spaces deafened
by unfamiliar lettering

Oxford

springing

heaventhralling
forsythiabursting
daylightsighting
violetsparkling
nightingalewaking
speckledeggspotting
leafmurmuring
scaldedfingersting
windbreathing
pillowbillowing
selfdelving
momentseeking
scentsoothing

Translated by: Tom Wachtel

the mystery of time

in the solitude of a silent garden
spring snowdrops
wake Socrates
from his dream of a dialogue

he makes a covenant
with eternity's evanescent closure
forged with
fragile cobwebs

it will keep secrets
enchanted
in the blackbird's song

socrates calls me in the middle of the night
he is crying

lebanese cedar

we're looking for shade
at Forty Hall
old cedar in the distance
will lend shelter
it has spread its branches for two hundred and fifty years

who brought the tree here from Lebanon
maybe as an act of love
maybe intoxicated by the scent of the moment
maybe a wanderer thirsty for memories

this will remain a mystery forever...

regent's park

he proposed to
invisible clouds
in Regent's Park.

and she
tangled by a rose muslin
circled by the sun
her golden feet
walked through the glass door

under the sky suspended
on a steel clock
at the top of Victorian towers

on a misty evening

dusk

behind the thicket of the night
he is still asleep
the invisible darkness
which trembles
lonely in his dreams

now the wings
of Icarus collapse
drawn by the night's yet invisible gravity

the last flash
of the sun goes away

illusion
is the eternity dormant in us

another alexandra palace spring

in the distance the city rumbles
pounding empty streets
shards of the day

there the mere illusion of light
here spring brings the sun

sweeping away the puddles
streams sparkle hiding in droplets of water
mistily entranced
we embrace

Translated by: Tom Wachtel

may

language braided with ivy
    touches the streams of rain

clouds thunder, swelled with the wind
they breathe heavily with the smell of forsythia and lilacs

the pond swings a silver fir tree

the time of sunny spaces is coming

birth

forgotten charm
neglected onion
and then a flower
a spring hope
first shoots

supposedly
we have no talent
supposedly
inspiration is born pure
uninvited

yet
it needs
a dust of burnt grass
of dried peat bogs

and suddenly
a bouquet
a tree
will bloom

a miracle

London April 28, 2005 – October 11, 2023

london rainbow

The London sun is setting, a rainbow appears, looks like nothing, but it opens the veil of secrecy. The cat still purrs, she wants more warm darkness: to captivate, hold, absorb, to repeat the adventures of the previous night. The silence pierces the saturated spaces and tea vapours in which the rays plunge. The city is now buzzing quietly, silenced by the cool sky. The sky peeks insidiously at the windows strained with silvery reflections. It reaches deep into cavernous secrets. The cat knows well that it is worth looking into the nothingness of the clouds for hours, his light airy purr says it all.

Close your hands, silence the heart, silence the desert winds. Let your imagination tell another fairy tale about the broken heart of the Little Prince and evil spirits coming every night. This is how the mountain of stories grows, the tip of an unsaid, banal, miserable, real life. The cat knows about it, she is waiting for another fairy tale, this doggy life is unknown to the red-haired aristocat.

Time is rushing, in a moment another underground stare. Faces of tired people, cold stalls. Kurds warming their hands, arranging pyramids of tomatoes, apples. It remains like this, for a dozen or so hours, or maybe for millennia; it does not matter whether here on London pavements, or somewhere far beyond the mountains and forests. And there, for sure, in the evening time, an old man still comes to visit a country cottage in the mountains and talks, looking at drawings imprinted on a skin, about princes from distant countries and their fair-haired sorceresses; about their blue eyes and frosty air. He ensures his audience that turquoise talismans are most effective in protecting against the unknown ...

summer in seaford

the sun sheds its golden drops
the sea devours them instantly
the sky shimmers

the day is snatched from another story
we're arriving, here at the end of the line
we convince ourselves that infinite space is an illusion
we walk through the small English town
to a tiny station, plaster falling unevenly off the wooden beams
before us the Channel gleams threateningly
in the distance a cliff plunges sharply into the sea
no chips, no ice cream, no candy floss
dead jellyfish glitter on the pebbles
the day passes lazily by
a ship silhouetted in grey against its face
on the beach a couple unfold deckchairs
wrinkled skin
they read the papers.
they seem unreal
postimpressionist faces
all nonchalant

we're heading back.
the cafes and restaurants are closed
who lives here at the end of the world

looking through photographs of the scandalous
Bloomsbury set
an old snapshot

a gaunt young woman and a man in deckchairs
they are reading the papers
what if the woman on the beach was a cousin of Virginia Woolf
who was the man
a poet
or one of her scandalous friends

the field gardens

can't cheat
the thickets of wildflowers in the city

painting the walls
welcoming glass clouds

and at night
silver sparks of stars
too distant

socrates is lost in anxiety

this is because of cold weather in May
and of today's cool philosophy

language braided with ivy

touches the streams of rain

clouds thunder, swelled with the wind

they breathe heavily with the smell of forsythia and lilacs

the pond swings a silver fir tree

in the cloud hidden thoughts of Socrates
he was afraid of his own thoughts
without touching the golden brightness
angelic paved the memory cells

Socrates was in the hospital
he returned
his heart now beats at an even pace
he made a fireplace burn again

the time of sunny spaces is coming

the camellias

deep in thought, streets of camellias
drowse
they wake up redolent of remembrance
open their flowers quickly stealing the sun's rays

they wait for the Hellenic messenger
for the aromatic waft of sapphire waves

day by day

against the gleaming rim
of the London sky

London 2009

low pressure in the land of the rain lovers

It's another New Year, I know how much is behind me; I know nothing about the future statistics of broken circles and sections. What will happen tomorrow, I don't want to know, it's just a grey fog, in contrast to today that is peacefully falling asleep under the purple pillow of dreams. I don't want to wait until tomorrow, I want to open the puffy bags of clouds, to warm up the frozen hands in the uncertain sun. I don't want to wander to the fairies stuck in the dirty windows and in the smoke of dying candles. It is only a temporary fleeting....
I allow myself to experience the low pressure. No patience, no time - do you know anything about this? We, with bags on our backs, we wonder what is really inside?
I will tell you a fairy tale, do not close your eyes. There was once a rich country famous for its vanishing fjords. The inhabitants lived well, so each year they wondered how to save the precious earth? However, it was not possible for them to rest, it was raining and raining. Winds blew, trees fell over, water flooded the houses. Inhabitants have learned to live and fight the elements. From generation to generation, they listened carefully the rhythm of falling drops.
One day, the sky resembled a hellish abyss, and the clouds changed their position at an incredibly fast pace, chased by the winds. Sometimes in the sky there appeared witches spinning in a crazy dance, wild creatures with huge maws. It was terrible, poignant. People locked in their little houses waited for the end. Streams of water flooded the windowpanes. It was the

witches who raged, splashing water from huge buckets all around. Buzzed, rumbled, blew, rumbled.
Andrew came to see me. He is a tall, bright-eyed Englishman. He sipped his tea with usual serenity. The conversation was not fluent, what was happening behind the window did not inspire a pleasant conversation. Andrew surreptitiously looked at the dripping window. Well - I thought - maybe he's afraid of these raging winds? He broke off the conversation, walked as if worried to the window, began to listen. After a while he asked:
- Can I open it?
- I allowed with no comment, although I was tormented by the question - what for?
He tilted his head outside and listened again.
A strange sound ... - he said.
Well, a little surprised I thought, what's strange about that? It's only rain ... Proud of his discovery, he shouted:
- The neighbours' gutter is leaking and flooding the right half of the house!
Everything became clear. Over the generations they have learned to listen to the rain. Now he predicts, announces, is the local postman for good and bad news about rain. He distinguishes the sound of dangerous and of correct droplets hitting! Amazing and how wise. To live on friendly terms with an ominous nature. Now I know how to identify a real Englishman - he can talk to the rain.

penzance

revival awakens in the night sweat
bubbly in the oceanic mud
drowning in the pirate chants

in the Celtic stone shelter from drops
in the lilac hair, the grass is thoughtful
shivering waves in Cornish sparks

the origins of the planet

eucalyptus silver is choked with stillness and slow destruction
it tempts with disorder
it's not supposed to be like this
this tranquillity is astonishing
it won't be like that

plants are looking for shelter
it wasn't supposed to be like this
eucalyptus shadow

it was not supposed to be this way
but it will definitely be different

London 2020

the ballad of penzance

slapstick
fringed
trumpeting
the ocean with a bang is reminding

with its glare seeks the castaways
Tristan and Isolde
with shanties of turquoise waves

threatens
to repentant boulders
to stone towers
conquered fortresses
Portuguese galleons

and they are astonished
shrouded in ballads
with an age of brass
with song they slumber

devon

ladder waves
shoot in waves
silvery sky
grayness

close summer floral
they leave the lid open
old trunks

on the bottom torn out
secrets

still in love with the sun

sunken
once upon a time in the fields

now
melt
in the London fog

sealed
a cobweb possessed

overgrown with grass
thicket bent

accustomed to breakups
are you still in love with the sun

in the english rythm

the clouds are looking lazily

my England allow the rain
my England does not allow the noise

these are births
and departures here

goodbyes
returns and joy
rays from the holidays
anointed
free…

thistle

we get up sunk
in the dew
devoted to the light
just for a moment

he whimpered
yesterday's thorn
will knock

open

confusion of thoughts
i put the buzzing gear into gear
abyss
oblivion

london jasmine

jasmine stimulates at dawn
wet smell
rough kiss
it's going to climb high
with white flower drops

in the morning
guts
and it makes sense
forgotten letters

cherries

Summer. A grey lane among some old cherries. Juicy white fruits fall, richly covering the fresh grass. It is always like this at this time of the year. The fruits attract herds of humming wasps.
The sweet smell of decaying balls attracts vermin. This is the most beautiful sight.

But Grandma didn't like those old, humpbacked trees. Each time in June, she repeated emphatically: only trouble, they attract wasps, they would bite the children…

Insects grew in our eyes, became monstrous, wild animals.
Yes, a neighbour added, last year they had bitten my granddaughter in the eyelid, we went to the hospital.

What is it for, these stories growing menacingly in the minds, filling the imagination of the audience, creating new myths?

And these are just innocent cherries. White, of unusual beauty, with delicate pink cheeks.
I grabbed handfuls, swallowed greedily, one, another, a third, and another.
Watch out for the wasps!
Grandma, the lady on the estate, noblewoman in Podlasie region in Eastern Poland, full of meadows and marshes. She hardened like that old cherry tree.

One day she will cut down a twisted, barky trunk, and June will never begin again.

About the author

Anna Maria Mickiewicz is a poet, writer, editor, translator, and publisher. Founder of the publishing house Literary Waves. Anna moved from Poland to California, and then to London. She is a member of the English Pen and Polish PEN Club. Her poetic works have appeared in the United States, UK, Australia, Canada, Poland, Mexico, Italy, Bulgaria, Hungary, Salvador, India, Chile, Peru. Honored with the Gloria Artis medal for Merit to Culture by the Polish Ministry of Culture, the Cross of Freedom and Solidarity, and The Joseph Conrad Literary Prize (USA).

In the 1980s, she co-edited the independent magazine Wywrotowiec (The Subversive) issued by the Inter-University Committee of Defence of Political Prisoners, in Poland. Since then, her articles have been published in many national and foreign magazines. She served as the chair of the California State Poetry Society Literary

Award Jury and the Jury of the International Literary Award of K. M. Anthru in India, the Jury of the Joseph Conrad Award (USA) and the Chapter of the Garden of Poetry Medal (London). She belongs to several London poetry groups, including: Enfield Poets, The Highgate Society's Poetry Group, Exiled Writers Ink. She co-edited and reformed the London literary journal Pamiętnik Literacki (Literary Diary). She cooperates with the American publishing house Dreammy Little City (Orlando) and prepared periodic poetry and literary anthologies. Together with University College London, with the participation of international poetry groups, she conducted poetry meetings as part of the UNESCO World Poetry Day - European Literary Dialogues. With the British translator Noel Clark, she participated in the creation of the Eagle and Lion exhibition, which was presented during Queen Elizabeth II's visit to Poland in March 1996. For many years she worked as a foreign correspondent for Polish press, describing cultural and literary events in Great Britain.

Acknowledgments

I would like to thank you to the authors Steve Rushton and David Clark for their valuable comments.
The Mystery of Time and Other Poems (USA)
London Manuscript (UK)